Meditation: Simple Guide to Beginning Practice

Brian Trzaskos
Eric Trzaskos

Authors and Publishers Note

Before following any advice or exercises contained in this book, it is recommended that you consult your doctor if you suffer from any health problems or special conditions, or are in any doubt as to their suitability. Neither the authors nor the publisher can accept responsibility for any injuries or damage incurred as a result of following the exercises in this book, or using any of the meditation techniques that are mentioned herein.

ISBN-13: 978-1463509729

To anyone seeking a small slice of health and energy, peace and quiet, clarity and focus...

Meditation, it's not what you think...

Contents

Contents 4

Why Another Guide To Meditation? 5

Why Meditate? 6

Let's Meditate 9

Abdominal Breathing 13

Pitfalls & Bridges.. 16

Developing A Regular Practice.................................... 24

Enjoy Your Way 30

Appendix A: Physiology of Stress and the Relaxation Response
.... 31

Appendix B: Creating Your Personal Anchoring Thought Form Worksheet... 39

References.. 41

Notes.. 42

Why Another Guide To Meditation?

You might do a quick search on the Internet and find literally thousands of books on meditation. These books range in focus from medical and psychological, sports to spiritual, relaxation to religion, and more. All of these books have value; yet what we find in working both with new meditators and during introduction to meditation workshops is that less is more. People just want to know how to get started: the basic practice and the most common hurdles. Often times we recommend some of our favorite resources, yet find ourselves giving caveats to each recommendation as well. Many meditation guides get very detailed and complicated rather rapidly. Yet, paradoxically, meditation is the simplest thing to do.

It is our intent to introduce you to the simplicity inherent in meditation, give you the basics up front and invite you to begin experiencing for yourself what meditation is. We offer further information in the appendix and in upcoming, subsequent guides in this series. We do our best to refrain from editorializing, allowing you to get oriented here, using it as a springboard to a deeper and/or more specific practice.

At the end of the day ALL the reading only informs you. Meditation has been practiced and written about for thousands of years. There is no new content or revelation to understand or write about meditation, it can only be packaged in different forms. While reading and studying help guide and inform you, it is only through your direct experience that you truly come to KNOW something for yourself.

> Meditation is explored through your own direct experience.

Why Meditate?

Tune The Mind & Self

All symphony musicians take a few moments to tune their instruments before they play and in doing so tune themselves to the instruments at the same time. Then, they each tune their own instrument to all the other instruments and in turn tune to all the other musicians. They do this each and every time to play in beautiful harmony and create wonderful music. In meditation you learn to tune your instrument, your mind: so powerful, so incredible, so often unchecked. As you continue your practice you come into harmony with your own mind, allowing creativity and receptivity to flow. With continued practice your newfound harmony extends to others, communicating, inspiring and collaborating, in simple and profound ways.

In many ways meditation practice is like learning how to build and flex our mental/emotional muscles. The tools that we naturally develop by simply sitting quietly can be used to help our daily lives become more effective, enjoyable, and peaceful. Just as an athlete trains in the gym to become more successful in competition, we retrain our minds and provide ourselves repeated experiential knowing in meditation to become more successful at life – in however *you* would like to define and measure success.

People typically become interested in and ultimately begin practicing meditation for at least one of three fundamental reasons: physical, mental/emotional, or spiritual. Interestingly, no matter why someone begins a meditation practice, he or she will experience benefits in all areas of his or her physical, mental/emotional, and spiritual life.

> Why are you interested in meditation?

Physical

In the physical realm people may begin meditating because they've heard it can, among other things, lower blood pressure, decrease muscle and back pain, lower cholesterol, and reduce anxiety and stress. In fact, multiple studies have shown that practicing meditation regularly benefits the immune system, the cardiovascular system, and increases the speed of physical healing.

We all know how stress and anxiety feel in our bodies; our heart races, blood pressure rises, and muscles tighten. Chronic stress has been linked to nearly every common degenerative condition in our society. If you are interested in more information on the physiological effects of the stress response and the relaxation response visit the appendices.

Mental / Emotional

Mentally we may have approached meditation to calm our overactive minds. Have you ever laid down to sleep, very tired, perhaps even exhausted, only to be subjected to a relentless onslaught of thoughts, images, and internal dialog? In times like these the ability to consciously calm the mind, separate from the mind, anytime you desire would be a very powerful gift indeed.

Emotionally an individual may seek meditation to help alleviate anxiety, depression, or anger. So many of us experience work stress, anxiety about our finances, and tension in the home. In a sense, our emotions are where the physical and spiritual meet in our bodies; and of course this can lead to many experiences ranging from tumult to ecstasy. Emotions are a primary manner of interacting with the world and each other. Meditation can teach us to become more accepting of who we already are emotionally so that we can observe and experience our emotions more fully and therefore interact more purposefully in the world.

Spiritual

In addition to the physical and emotional, some people seek out meditation to create more depth in the meaning of their life and to strengthen their connection with forces beyond our physical world. By nature, the spiritual aspect of our self is difficult to describe because it exists in a place beyond words. Practicing meditation offers us an opportunity to silently experience our spiritual self directly; and, as a result, trust, faith, and compassion naturally blossom.

Let's Meditate

Though there are thousands of meditation techniques, in general they boil down to three basic types: concentration, mindfulness and centering prayer.

Concentration meditation is about learning to focus attention using your breath, a word, sound, vision, or other anchoring thought form.

Mindfulness meditation is about opening attention to your present experience. With regular practice, mindfulness can be experienced with all activities such as working, playing, house chores, and even dreaming.

The idea of centering prayer is to open yourself to the presence of God, in whatever "God" means to you. This may be an experience of feeling complete, "at one with", an acute sense of unity, gratitude, and/or love. It doesn't necessarily imply a religious connotation. Practically speaking, a centering prayer practitioner uses an anchoring thought form or concept to create a connection with the *feeling* of sitting in the divine, and, again uses that anchor to return and reconnect when the mind wanders.

The following is a simple, beginner meditation. Technically it is a combination of concentration and mindfulness meditation.

For you, it can begin to:
• Make you more aware of yourself and various aspects of your "self"
• Directly introduce you to the basic pitfalls we all meet in our meditation practice

> Meditation is
> simply the intention
> to focus our
> attention.

9

1. Sit quietly and comfortably with spine straight.

This can be in a chair with feet on the floor, cross-legged on the floor or a cushion.

Ideally, there are limited or no distractions. As appropriate, close the door, turn off your phone, and ask not to be disturbed.

2. Choose an anchoring thought form

An anchoring thought form is a word/phrase, object, or visualization that you repeat and return to when your attention wanders.

These thought forms help you go deeper into meditation and to continue the meditation practice more consistently, but they are not absolutely required to begin meditating.

See the appendices for a worksheet and examples on creating your own personalized thought form.

Choose a personalized thought form that means something to you. Find a word or phrase that makes you feel relaxed, happy, inspired, flowing and/or whole; this will guide you deeper into meditation and because it feels good, you are more likely to continue practicing.

Abdominal Breathing – An alternative to an anchoring thought:

An anchoring thought form is a great tool to begin experiencing meditation and observing the mind's activities; however, using a thought form is actually using the mind to help focus the mind. So what happens when the mind is moving at a rate of thought with such ferocity that you can barely keep still? Well, let's take the mind out of the meditation and focus solely on our breath through a simple abdominal breathing exercise. You can use abdominal breathing as a pre-meditation exercise or for your whole sitting session. Coming up we'll talk about breathing in more detail.

3. Observe your breathing, relax, and repeat your anchoring thought

Focus 25% of your attention on your breath. Allow yourself to feel the sensation of breathing without trying to change the breath. Notice the body breathing.

On exhale, say out loud or think internally your anchoring thought form. If you do not have one, focus on your breath with all your attention.

4. Passive Attitude

When your mind wanders (and it will), gently return your attention to your practice (breath and anchoring thought) with a smile ☺

The most common misconception of those new to meditation is that they are doing it wrong, that their mind is too chaotic and they are not doing it 'right' or 'well' and not 'getting anywhere' or 'gaining the benefits'.

Return to your practice and smile, you are perfect.

> The most common misconception: new meditators think they are doing it wrong.

5. 5min – 20min / day; 1-2 times each day

Allow yourself to start small and increase your practice times as you become more comfortable. 5-20 minutes each day is a very reasonable amount of time to change your life immeasurably. Thank yourself as you finish each session, acknowledging the time and energy you gave and dedicated to yourself.

6. Start Today! Try a 30-day experiment...

We've covered the basics and the only thing left to do is to start sitting. Make an agreement with yourself that no matter what else comes up in your life for the next 30 days, you will create the time and space necessary to meditate daily. If you're really into it, keep a journal of your 30-day practice noting whether or not you meditated as well as any particular observations and changes in awareness.

It doesn't have to be your version of perfect, whether that means sitting at the same time every day or building your practice duration to a certain length of time.

Simply start sitting.

Get comfortable, breath deeply, and begin…

Abdominal Breathing

Abdominal breathing is a fairly simple technique to simultaneously relax and energize the body and mind. Abdominal breathing can be used as an alternative to a mental device / anchoring thought form (see Let's Meditate #2) or as the center of your attention for your sitting session.

In the western world breathing is thought of as a mechanical way to transfer oxygen into our lungs and carbon dioxide out of them. While this is mechanically true, traditional medicine practices all over the globe consider breathing in terms of energy transfer and as one of the most powerful ways to develop ideal health.

One of the most common problems with breathing in western society is

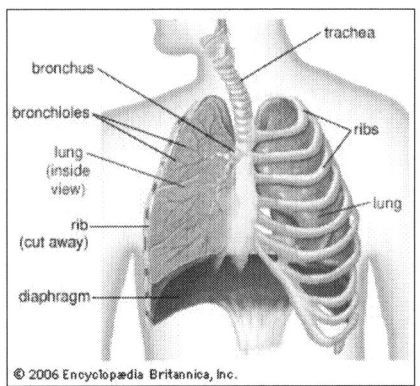

the tendency to chest-breathe and in effect we work very hard to fill the lungs against the inner wall of the ribs. This habit can be formed very early in life and has been attributed to the effects of chronic stress episodes. Indeed, when people are in a stress response their breathing becomes very rapid and shallow, using what are known as accessory muscles to breathe rather than the more efficient diaphragm.

Over time this style of respiration, known as upside down breathing, causes an oxygen deficit in the body and brain. The lungs are pyramid shaped and therefore contain more surface area for oxygen transfer at their base. When breathing occurs primarily in the chest about a teacup full of blood is oxygenated with

Oxygenate 5x more blood to the body and brain.

each breath. With abdominal, or belly breathing, roughly a liter of blood (5x more) receives oxygen with each breath. This huge difference in oxygen saturation means that your body and brain will receive five times the amount of oxygen with every abdominal breath. Considering that nerve tissue is very sensitive to oxygen deprivation and your brain is the largest recipient of blood in the body, it is no wonder that when people learn to belly breathe effectively they see an improvement in short term memory and cognitive thinking.

The other interesting thing that happens with chest breathing is that the blood chemistry changes causing it to become more acidic, which has been shown to provoke anxiety. The power of abdominal breathing can be felt by simply performing ten deep belly breaths that will cause the blood chemistry to neutralize and therefore minimize anxiety feelings and behaviors.

Lying Down Position

It is easy to learn abdominal breathing; actually we all did it quite naturally as children and still have those motor memories available to us if we choose to use them. Start by lying on your back with knees bent and feet flat on the floor. Place something on your abdomen like a book or stuffed animal. Take some relaxed breaths and notice the differences in movement between the chest and stomach. Ideally as you breathe in, your belly will rise and as you breathe out your belly will fall. There should be minimal movement in the chest and only at the end of the "in" breath, if at all. If this doesn't happen naturally then imagine a long tube extending from your nose all the way into the stomach. As you breathe inward through the nose, feel your stomach expand as air is pulled past the chest all the way into the abdomen.

Imagine that your stomach is a hot air balloon rising up with each in-breath and falling with each out-breath. Notice if that book or stuffed animal on your belly is moving up and down and how it relates to any movement in the chest. Spend as much time as you need to master this breathing technique in the lying down position.

Seated Position

When you feel very comfortable with abdominal breathing while lying down, move into a seated position in a straight-backed chair. Sit comfortably with a relaxed but erect spine. Place both hands, on your sides, below your rib cage with fingers facing to the front. Take a few relaxed breaths and again observe the relationship of movement between the chest and abdomen. Again visualize a long tube running from your nose to your belly, and with each in-breath bypass the chest bringing air all the way into the abdomen. Allow your belly to expand out and down while breathing in; pull your abdomen in and up while breathing out. For many it is more difficult to learn abdominal breathing while seated. If you get confused or frustrated simply return to lying on your back and practice breathing as previously described. It is very important to translate this breathing technique from lying down to sitting and even standing, where it can be used daily (standing in line at the grocery store, for example).

As a regular practice you may choose to set aside ten minutes each day for simple abdominal breathing. With practice you will also find that abdominal breathing can be successfully employed before, or even during, a stressful meeting and certainly any time during the day when you feel tense. It's a good thing breathing is socially acceptable...you can do it everywhere!

Pitfalls & Bridges

You've started your meditation practice, excellent!
In your own direct experience, within one or two sessions, you have
probably become keenly aware of at least one pitfall, if not them all.

Let's look at each pitfall and begin putting methods in place (a bridge) to
understand and move through them.

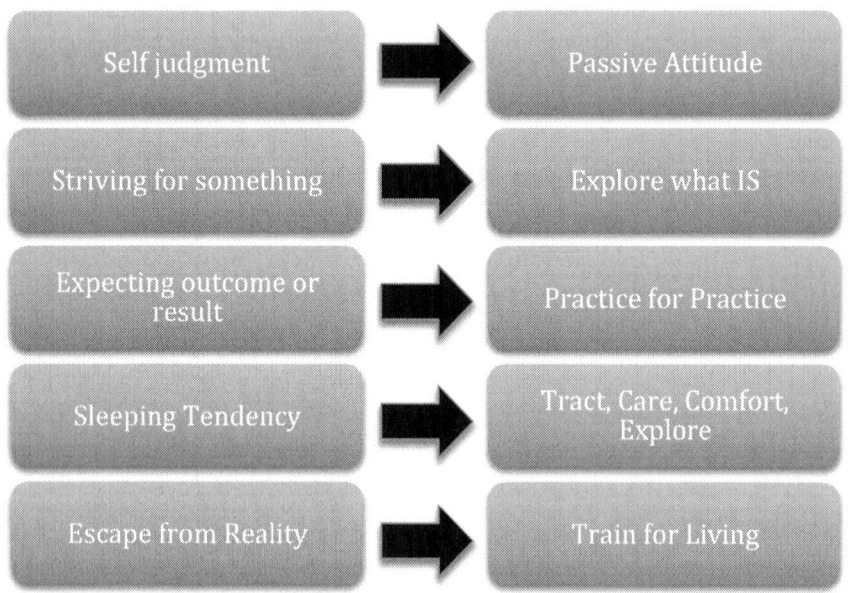

Pitfalls & Bridges

Self-Judgment → Passive Attitude

Remember, all beginning meditators have one thing in common…self-doubt (ie. they think they are doing it wrong; they are not deriving the physical benefit because their mind continues to wander, and everyone else must be doing better.)
This is where most folks lose patience, get frustrated and discontinue their sitting session or their practice entirely.

Also remember, everyone's mind wanders, usually within 2-5 seconds of focusing attention. Of course, the more you practice, the longer the gaps in the mind will become. The mind is very efficient at learning and building new pathways; it just needs to be taught and re-taught (reprogrammed).

The point is not to control the mind or try and make the mind go blank; but rather to simply return to the practice in a light-hearted manner. In fact, 'trying' to think no thoughts is an exercise in futility; it's not possible because the mind thinks thoughts. That's part of the mind's job, part of why we still exist and have evolved to the degree we have. A clear mind actually comes with letting go of everything, watching / witnessing…and practice.

> Meditation is sincere, but not serious.

As we get frustrated, judge our practice, and even berate ourselves we get wrapped around those very thoughts of frustration and judgment. This is often called fusion or misidentification with the thoughts. When this happens we are no longer focusing attention on the breath and/or the anchoring thought, but rather our center of attention has shifted to the very thoughts and frustration that is leading our attention away. But it's interesting, isn't it? When you notice that your attention has drifted and you begin to judge yourself, ask yourself "Who or what noticed that I drifted? Who or what is noticing that I am beginning to judge my self?"

From a physiological perspective, when we self-judge, we engage a stress response (fight or flight), that creates anxious, reactionary feelings; practice isn't over because as quickly as attention shifts away, it can shift back. In fact, within your practice you will physically feel the muscles and energy in your body change when your attention drifts and you self-judge. This is a wonderful, on-board indicator, a gentle reminder, your body telling you that you have drifted and to bring your attention back. It's that simple.

Your mind is not your enemy; it is only doing what it has been taught and conditioned to do up to now. Knowing this allows you to return your attention to your breathing or anchoring thought with acceptance, openness, and compassion with a smile. Guide your attention back as you would a loving child, a dear friend, or a trusted colleague.

A word on "passive" - in our society the word 'passive' has a negative connotation, one of being weak and victimized. Here we consider passive to mean inactive, uninvolved, and non-participatory with respect to the mind's activities. That is, we observe and watch the mind's activities, the thoughts, images, and inner dialog as if watching cars passing down the street outside our home or as wispy clouds passing across the clear sky of mind. We are not trying to stop the thoughts or even change the thoughts; we are simply observing thoughts. What we are changing is our relationship to the thoughts.

> Passive means 'inactive and unresponsive' with respect to the mind's activities.

When we consistently, routinely, and gently return to our practice without getting wrapped around our thoughts and without drama...with a smile, wonder, even humor, the amazing magic of meditation happens and our physical, mental/emotional, and spiritual health improve.

Striving For Something → Exploring What IS

Be aware that the striving mind can turn a meditation practice into a means to get things done.

While you may begin exploring and continuing meditation for healthy motives, when one sits in meditation 'trying' to derive those benefits, those benefits become even more elusive because you are no longer truly meditating. This is one of the paradoxes of meditation.

Striving can come in obvious forms such as wanting to lower blood pressure and reduce anxiety, or subtler forms such as wanting to control the mind and live in peace, or many variations in-between. Either way, the mind has entered meditation with an attitude of control and manipulation, with a purpose, an agenda. As your mind attempts to capture your attention and lead it away, practice accepting the content of the mind (thoughts, images, etc), allowing the content to pass by without attaching to it.

When you sit in meditation, it is an incredible opportunity to explore for yourself what happens when the mind has nothing to do. Practice accepting what IS, within your practice, as you bring yourself back to center.

> What happens when the mind has nothing to do?

Trust your body to inherently know what corrections to make; take your hands off the wheel and explore for yourself in your own direct experience.

Expecting An Outcome → Practice For Practice

Many times people think that during every meditation something magical and moving will happen. They expect to see things like beautiful colors, have out of body experiences, receive inspirational ideas and profound insights, or walk away with such deep calm and presence that the Dalai Lama

> Meditation is not work; it is a form of play.

himself would be in awe. While these things, and others far more subtle and profound, can be experienced throughout the tenure of meditation practice, there is no guarantee they will. This is another paradox of meditation.

Very often we are fixated on an outcome or some current situation and miss the infinite possibilities that continually present themselves. We are simply blinded by our expectations and attitudes. Approach meditation with no expectations or desires; sit with courage and openness to whatever may come and experience it fully in each moment.

Meditation is a state of grace and through consistent practice wondrous things can happen. Considering this, it is important to come to every meditation period with a heart open to any possibility, to directly explore through your own witnessing the leading edge of your experience. Profound shifts in consciousness and awareness may occur when nothing seems to happen at all.

The following quote on meditation by Saint Francis de Sales can apply to many aspects of meditation; in this case, it speaks subtly to practicing for the sake of practice:

"If the heart wanders or is distracted, bring it back to the point quite gently...and even if you did nothing during the whole of your hour but bring your heart back, though it went away every time you bring it back, your hour would be very well employed."

Sleeping Tendency → Tract, Care, Comfort, Explore

Your meditation practice will undoubtedly mingle with sleep, especially when beginning meditation or when returning to meditation after a break in your practice.

Fundamentally, the body has been conditioned to know sleep as a time when the mind lets go and both mind and body relax. Is this not what happens when you 'go' to sleep? When beginning or returning to

> Meditation is falling awake.

meditation the body simply goes into this old program, not yet knowing a state of consciousness where awareness AND relaxation coexist. With the suggestions below and some time, effort, and energy on your part you will reset the program and rebuild the tract.

1. **Are you getting enough sleep?**
   Two thirds of us are sleep deprived, so as the body relaxes it decides to give us what it needs...sleep. Everyone's sleep requirements vary, but a good rule of thumb is 7-8 hours a day. Take care of yourself. No matter how much more you think you are getting done without proper sleep your efficiency and ability 'to do' let alone 'to be' is reduced.

2. **When are you meditating?**
   • Refrain from practice after meals as blood is in the stomach rather than in the brain.
   • Morning meditations after some chores or light exercise will bring wonderful energy to your practice and permeate itself through the rest of your walking and waking day.
   • Meditating after light-moderate exercise can also help to energize you through your afternoon or evening meditations. Also, attempting meditation after strenuous exercise may be counter-productive because the body's responses are focused on activation rather than relaxation.

21

3. **How comfortable are you?**
   • While you want to be sitting comfortably with spine straight and wearing comfortable clothing, if you're too comfortable you may just doze off. This doesn't mean you have to wrap yourself into exotic yoga positions or pain yourself; it simply means choosing a posture where you can be relaxed yet awake and not falling into your favorite easy chair or lying on the couch.
   • Environmentally, is your room too warm or stuffy? Is the ambient noise too neutral or white (i.e. monotone fan, air flow, or soft motor)?
   • Are you well hydrated? Many people are under-hydrated, causing lethargy. On a related note, don't forget to use the toilet before sitting for longer periods.

4. **Are you reacting to anxiety?**
   Many beginning meditators are so unused to 'being' with themselves that it actually causes a mild anxiety. Initially when practicing many people do not experience meditation; they experience their own mind, which can be extremely unpleasant at times. This is very common and very natural. The body and mind are simply reacting to the discomfort and temporarily shut down. Remember to have courage and openness with your meditation. Allow yourself to explore, for yourself, in your own direct experience what is happening in you, to you, and around you without needing to control, judge, or manipulate. Explore.

Escape From Reality → Train For Living

Remember that meditation is not an escape from reality. It is indeed valuable to enter silence for daily healing and respite; however at some point you need to participate in life (get back into the game).

As mentioned earlier, meditation practice is like learning how to build and flex our mental/emotional muscles; the tools that we naturally develop by simply sitting quietly can be used to help our daily lives become more effective, enjoyable, and peaceful.

> Being present, enjoy living more richly and fully.

Just as an athlete trains in the gym to become more successful in competition, we retrain our mind and provide ourselves repeated experiential knowing in meditation to become more successful at life – in however *you* would like to define and measure success.

Although we sit in silence, observe, explore, and practice, we are still part of this physical world, an integral part. We still exist and interact; this is part of being human.
A famous Zen proverb reminds us, "Before enlightenment chop wood and carry water. After enlightenment chop wood and carry water." Essentially this teaching reminds us to take the lessons we learn from meditation and apply them to the most routine tasks of our daily existence, turning the outwardly mundane into the inwardly sublime.

Developing A Regular Practice

The most important thing is that you are meditating, that you are giving yourself the time and opportunity to sit. This is wonderful! Ideally you are meditating in a way that is most enjoyable and repeatable for you. Developing a regular meditation practice will help with this, bringing more enjoyment and consistency to your practice while allowing you to move deeper into your meditations. Developing a regular practice will also require some structure and discipline until it becomes a natural and valuable part of your life routine. You may have to experiment over a couple weeks to discover what works best for you. The point here is to develop consistency around your practice. One or all of the following concepts will help in designing your meditation practice.

> Meditation can be the most enjoyable experience of your day, your life!

Set Time of Day

Finding and setting a consistent time of day to meditate is very important. Finding a regular time that works best for you is one of the quickest and easiest ways to develop consistency around your practice and will begin to bring the mind-body into harmony. Take notice, perhaps even journal, on how your perspectives and interactions change from simply having a set time to ground and re-center yourself each day.

For practical and energetic reasons the best time to practice meditation is in the morning before breakfast. Morning symbolizes a new beginning allowing you to set specific intentions and for the energy of your meditation to permeate throughout the day.

Not everyone who wants to meditate will have the opportunity in the morning to set a consistent time. Look for those times when the house is quiet and free of chaotic influence (5-20min). Also try to meditate before or at least 2 hours after a meal.

Let's be honest though…no matter how consistent you attempt to be, your routine will inevitably be interrupted. And no matter how ideal you want to have a specific time, it will not always be available, if at all. Even if the times vary it's most important that you create the 5-20min at some point each day to sit with your "self" in practice.

Set A Space

Seasoned practitioners will find that he or she can meditate almost anywhere, however when beginning a practice it might be best to choose a special place to "sit". Ideally, this place would be used only for the purpose of meditation, but not mandatory. Choosing a consistent space and place that you consider special is beneficial. You may choose to include a small table or shelf covered with a particular cloth, arranged with small statues or photos that inspire you. Also consider having plants, a fountain, your favorite chair, cushion, blankets, or an ambient noisemaker. Perhaps you have certain clothing that is comfortable and special for you.

> This is your time for you.

If you have a cell phone turn it off or place it in airplane mode and on vibrate (lest a reminder jar you from your meditation). For home phones, turn the ringer down or unplug them if you must. This is your time for you. Many of us are so uncomfortable being 'cut off' from everything and everyone, dominated by neediness, worry or 'what if' or completely over stimulated. We have forgotten what 'our time for ourselves' even means or feels like.

It is unwise and usually unsuccessful to practice meditation in a place where you often do other things like sit at the computer or in front of the television. Our mind-body is constantly taking cues from our surroundings on what is expected. Even before we sit at the computer to work our body is shifting into gear for that task.

When you create a dedicated space for meditation, your mind-body will also fall into this routine and even as you approach that special place your disposition will shift to relaxation and ease.

The Proper Position

Getting comfortable is critical so that the body can release tension and move towards a state of alert relaxation. Many people choose to sit cross-legged on a cushion; however it is equally effective to sit in a straight-backed chair with an erect, yet relaxed spine. Place your feet flat on the floor, maintain a straight spine, allow your head to balance above your shoulders, and gently place your hands on your lap with palms facing up or down. While a lying posture is assumed for some yoga positions and guided meditations (i.e. body scan) it is not recommended for beginning meditators as it predisposes one to falling asleep.

Pre Practice Routine

Your body will move more quickly into a meditative state with increased practice and when you employ a pre practice routine to signal your mind-body that it is time to meditate. Some people choose certain breathing techniques like the simple abdominal breathing that you've already learned.

Others choose a simple stretching routine such as a yoga sun salute, back rotations, other stretching or Tai Chi / Qi Gong. A morning routine can be a few simple morning tasks that provide easy stretching movement and a sense of completion preceding a formal period of sitting. Reading a short passage from an inspirational reference may also set an underlying intention for your meditation that allows you to go deeper.

The mind settles down with routine and repetition. The more consistent the practice, the less the mind will resist opening to the experience of meditation. In fact, you may find yourself looking forward to meditating more than anything else...meditation can be one of the most enjoyable experiences of your day and life.

Ending Your Practice

How do you know when to finish your practice? While the essence of your practice can be carried with you all day, your actual sitting time will come to an end at some point. Seasoned practioners inherently know when it is time to finish their practice session and "come back".

As a beginning meditator you can use a timer that is purchased especially for meditation or simply use one on your phone or computer (both can be configured to use as a timer while remaining silent for calendar/task notifications and in airplane mode). If possible, choose a timer chime that is relatively soothing, inspiring or neutral. We don't want to be jarred from our meditation, just gently reminded that it is time to come back.

If you don't have any means to time your practice, choose how long you will sit and simply meditate for as long as you feel is appropriate and see how well you matched up to your desired time. Take note and have fun with it. You will be surprised at how long, short, or spot-on you will be in your estimations and how it directly relates to the amount of awareness in your practice.

Post Practice Routine

It is also very helpful to consistently close your practice.

Before getting up you can take an extra 30-60 seconds to close your meditation with any of the following:
* Thanking yourself for the time devoted to you
* Visualizing and feeling an inspirational figure
* Having compassion for yourself, specific others, and the world
* Visualizing or creating an intention for your day
* Simply having gratitude for the day and this gift of life

As you begin moving again your post-practice routine, may again include light stretching, yoga, Tai Chi, self-massage or reading favored passages.

With the post-practice routine we continue to settle and reprogram the mind with routine, repetition and consistency in a manner that supports our intentions, lives, and interactions for the entire day.

Enjoy Your Way

We know there is plenty of information in here, even for a beginner's guide, to help you start and continue a wonderful meditation practice. It was our intent to give you a balance of practical simplicity, get you meditating, answer your immediate questions, and keep you meditating. Yet it doesn't scratch the surface of the immensity of information available on meditation. All the information is no substitute for sitting down and exploring your own silent spaces, for yourself, in your own direct experience. This is where true learning will occur, on the edge of the known and unknown within you. We wish you the best on your way and in your practice. Have fun.

Please contact us with any questions, feedback, or to share...we love to hear from everyone on their own, individual journeys.

Brian Trzaskos
www.ascentwellness.com

Eric Trzaskos
www.meditationsimpleguide.com

Look for upcoming guides in our **Simple Guide** series.

Appendix A: Physiology of Stress and the Relaxation Response

Stress Response Physiology

Our nervous system is basically divided into two parts, the Somatic and Autonomic divisions. While there is tremendous overlap and complexity in these systems it can simply be organized this way:

Somatic Division	Autonomic Division
Brain	Sympathetic
Spinal Cord	Parasympathetic
Peripheral Nerves	Glands
Electrical	Hormonal

We use the somatic division of the nervous system when we want to move our muscles or do anything consciously like getting in and out of chairs, walking, and brushing our teeth. In contrast, our autonomic branch is working all the time, mostly beyond our conscious control, to keep our bodies in a state of internal balance. This internal balance is based largely on the constant evaluation of our surroundings and ourselves; especially in terms of whether or not we feel threatened. Threat need not be physical to evoke a powerful response from the autonomic nervous system; many times threat to our ideas and sense of self create the most destructive patterns in our bodies.

The autonomic nervous system is further divided into two branches called the sympathetic and parasympathetic systems. These are more commonly called the "Fight or Flight" and "Rest and Digest" responses.

Homeostasis: a <u>dynamic</u> balance between the two autonomic branches.

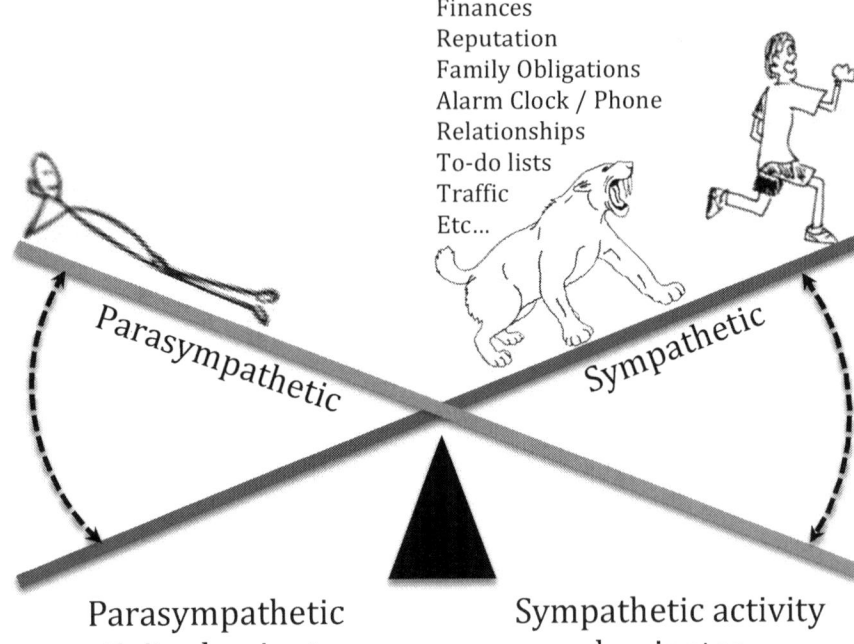

Finances
Reputation
Family Obligations
Alarm Clock / Phone
Relationships
To-do lists
Traffic
Etc...

Parasympathetic activity dominates:
Rest and Digest

Sympathetic activity dominates:
Fight or Flight

Fight or Flight (Stress Response)

Let's look back a few million years to our great, great, great ancestor; for now let's call him ancient man. Was ancient man stressed? He dealt with periods of drought and famine, as well as large predators that he would engage from time to time. So while he was stressed at times, it was in a much different way than we are today.

When ancient man crossed paths with a saber-toothed tiger an immediate change in his physiology would occur, solely geared towards survival. This physiological shift in response to danger or threat is commonly referred to as the "Fight or Flight" response. Ancient man's blood pressure and heart rate would jump higher so that oxygen could more rapidly be delivered to his muscles, his blood sugar would increase for instant energy, blood clotting would be enhanced, reflexes would sharpen, and muscle tension would increase exponentially. Below is a list of physiological effects as a result of the stress response:

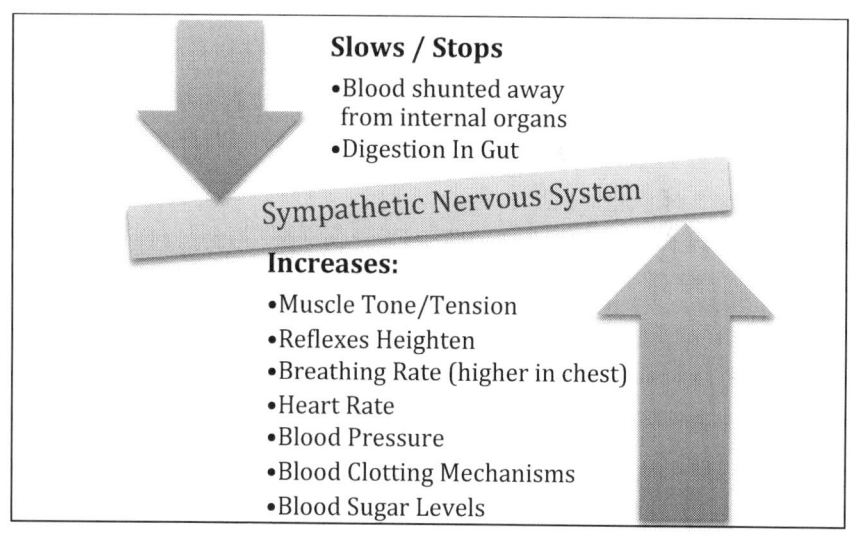

Slows / Stops
- Blood shunted away from internal organs
- Digestion In Gut

Sympathetic Nervous System

Increases:
- Muscle Tone/Tension
- Reflexes Heighten
- Breathing Rate (higher in chest)
- Heart Rate
- Blood Pressure
- Blood Clotting Mechanisms
- Blood Sugar Levels

Effects of Stress Response

The more efficiently that these things would happen, the more likely that ancient man wouldn't become somebody else's lunch. Those ancient folk with weak stress responses probably didn't live very long, and those with robust stress responses went on to reproduce. So in some ways, we are the result of a long lineage of people who were exceptionally good at becoming stressed.

The glaring difference between ancient man's stressful experience and stress in modern times is the length of time that stressors are allowed to carry on. Ancient man would have either been eaten or escaped in a matter of minutes, using all of those physiological adaptations to perform intense physical activity and save his hide. Today we tend to remain in, or link, multiple stress episodes daily, weekly, monthly throughout the year stimulated by our state of finances, health, family, and/or job situation to name a few.

Effects of Stress Response	
Short Term	**Long Term**
Immune Function Stops	High Blood Pressure
Brain Cell Creation Stops	Heart Disease / Atherosclerosis
Older Brain Cell Degeneration Increases	Diabetes
Anxiety Increases	Chronic Anxiety
Reactionary Behavior Increases	Chronic Depression
Mental Capacity & Functioning Decrease	High Blood Sugar
Peripheral Vision Decreases	
Analytical / Creative Thinking Decreases	

Remember that "fight or flight" is triggered in response to a <u>perceived</u> threat; and what is more threatening to us than potentially losing our jobs, family, homes, or becoming ill. It is when stress responses are allowed to carry on for extended periods of time that chronic states of ill health such as high blood pressure, heart

> Fight or Flight is triggered by a perceived threat.

disease, and diabetes become a reality. In fact, this problem is so pervasive that most experts indicate that 75% of all doctors' visits in the US are unnecessary, due to an over engaged stress response, costing over $50B per year. There are more immediate effects of stress as well, that affect you within minutes of a stress response. These include immune system depression, the creation of new brain cells stopping, increased degeneration of older brain cells, increased anxiety, decreased mental capacity, and reactionary behavior.

While short bouts of stress lasting minutes to hours can actually improve immune function assuming they are 'run' out and dealt with effectively, the effects of chronic stress wreak havoc with our short term and long term health.

Rest and Digest (Relaxation Response)

After ancient man barely escapes from the saber tooth his heart rate begins to slow down, breathing becomes deeper, and muscle tension decreases. He may even feel grateful that he is still alive. Having 'run' out the stress response he returns to his tasks, collecting wood for shelter or foraging for food. The immediate threat gone, his body returns to inner balance so that it might function optimally in the present moment.

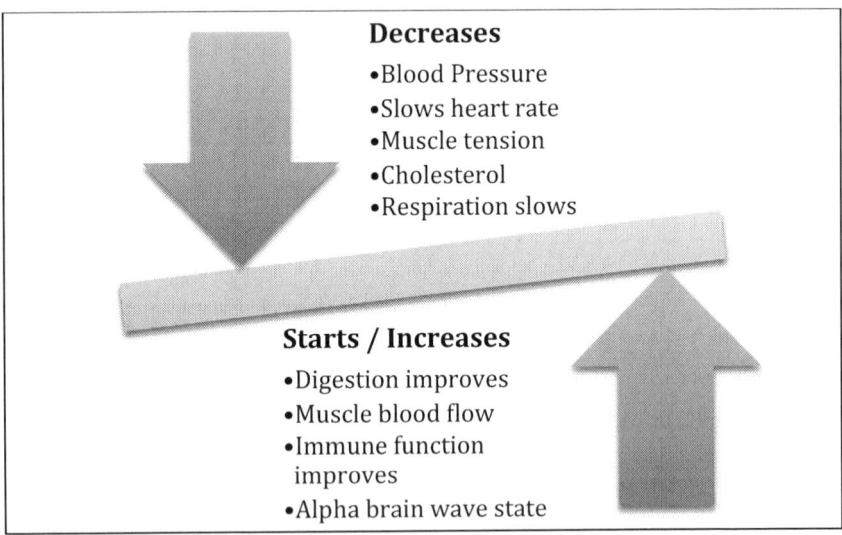

Decreases
- Blood Pressure
- Slows heart rate
- Muscle tension
- Cholesterol
- Respiration slows

Starts / Increases
- Digestion improves
- Muscle blood flow
- Immune function improves
- Alpha brain wave state

Effects of Relaxation Response

Unlike the ancient man scenario, our modern day stress is more commonly composed of small to moderate stress episodes throughout the day. Before getting out of bed what is the first thing you think of, is it your to-do list? Sometimes the alarm alone can cause our first stress episode of the day. Getting the kids off to school, the newspaper filled with stories of violence and the poor economic climate are additional episodes. Traffic, meetings, inboxes, deadlines, and workload can each cause subsequent stress episodes before heading back home to family obligations. None of these things by themselves are enough to induce a full-blown "fight or flight" response, but summed up they create enough tension in the body to cause disease and put you on a stress trend toward permanent hyper-metabolic states, permanent stress.

Here's the great news...our bodies are able to balance out the damaging effects of chronic stress through engagement of the parasympathetic nervous system, called the Relaxation Response. More than balancing the effects of stress; the Relaxation Response can put you on a relaxation trend toward consistent hypo-metabolic states, creative thinking, open mindedness, and more collaborative relationships.

The best part is, it's easy to elicit the Relaxation Response; you have everything you need with you at all times! You, your breath, your attention and 10-20min, 1-2 times a day (see Let's Meditate section).

Research has shown that healing becomes faster and more efficient when the relaxation response is activated regularly, and that it takes surprisingly little time each day to make fundamental changes in your health. Can you imagine breathing for just a few minutes in silence following a stress episode? You will be amazed at the immediate affects you notice, not to mention the long term ones.

Effects of Relaxation Response	
Short Term	**Long Term – Improve or Cure**
Immune Function Boosts	Blood Pressure
Brain Cell Creation Resumes	Heart Disease / Atherosclerosis
Brain Cell Overstimulation Ceases	Diabetes
Anxiety Decreases / Disappears	Chronic Anxiety
Proactive Behavior Increases	Chronic Depression
Mental Capacity & Functioning Increase	All Chronic Pain
Peripheral Vision Widens	Developing Cancer
Analytical / Creative Thinking Increases	Symptoms of Cancer & HIV
	Ulcers
	Sexual Dysfunction
	High Blood Sugar
	Many, Many More…

Appendix B: Creating Your Personal Anchoring Thought Form Worksheet

Directions:

• List 3-5 renewal moments that mean the most to you, those you can easily feel and associate with. Be sure to read the suggestions below for guidance.

• Renewal Moments are when:
  • You feel whole, in the moment, flowing
  • Your energy body is in a state of harmony; your batteries are recharging
  • You are smiling, welling with gratitude
  • You experience a belief, routine, or comfort action that makes you feel good and "at one with…"
  • You feel joy petting an animal, playing with a child, being in "the zone", or at ease out in nature

• Consider the different areas of your life where you may feel joyful or enriched. A surprising renewal moment may be found in one of these seven areas of life.
  • Occupational
  • Family / Intimacy
  • Financial
  • Health
  • Mental / Emotional
  • Social
  • Spiritual

• For each renewal moment come up with 1-7 words / phrase that you can associate with the renewal moment.
  • The words should be simple, distilled, and able to say with one

39

breath cycle
- Examples are: Arriving home, Be Present, Now, One
- Words may include an object or visualization
- You can refine it later, but once you get <u>something you like</u>, stick with it for a while, see and feel what happens before rushing to change it. Remember, consistency and routine settles the mind.

Renewal Moment		Convert to Thought Association
1.	→	1.
2.	→	2.
3.	→	3.
4.	→	4.
5.	→	5.

References

Benson, Herbert MD. *The Relaxation Response.* NY: William Morrow Company, 1975

Hendricks, Gay PHD. *Conscious Breathing.* NY: Bantam Books, 1995

Borysenko, Joan PHD. *The Beginners Guide to Meditation.* Hay House, 2006

Fontana, David PHD. *Learn to Meditate.* London: Duncan Baird Publishers, 1999

Benson, Herbert MD. *Beyond The Relaxation Response.* NY: Times Books, 1984

Harris, Russ MD. *ACT Made Simple.* CA: New Harbinger Publications, 2009

Boyatzis, Richard PHD. *Resonant Leadership: Inspiring Others Through Emotional Intelligence.* More Than Sound, 2009

Adyashanti. *True Meditation.* CO: Sounds True, Inc, 2006

Notes

Made in the USA
San Bernardino, CA
26 April 2016